Thank you for buying a Papercute™. Explore the full collection at
www.papercutenotebooks.com

THIS JOURNAL BELONGS

TO

_____

August 25, 2019

Dear Diary,

Liz loves her life today! She did all the things and drank all the drinks. She lived her best life!! This new journal will document all the fun and adventures for the rest of 2019.

Liz's goals for the week:
- have fun
- Stop caring so much about what others think
- Don't drunk text boys
- "Live your best life"
- Love yourself because we all love you!! ♡

XOXO- Christie

Thank you for giving me
an amazing day,
I met you and you were
a gentleman cine y(?) wht
home evan tha thats not
what i wanted- but you
were kind calm and sweet
to the touch. You made me
smile snothg you made
me want more. I hope
I get to see you again
soon (tomarow)
I might be convinced
that im worty agun
you touched my nec
in the sens tht
you left without me
getting the order
see you soon

August 26

More sore then I would
have been if I had
gone to spin class
Too much Dragging
if thats possible.

My Poke turned out great
Paddle Boaring was
great. And who can
complain about Adult
Capri Sun.

Also Kobe and I are
celebrating national dog
day tomorow.

Today i learned Silence is
nice...

Made in the USA
San Bernardino, CA
23 August 2019